The Rainy Day Activity Book

The Rainy Day Activity Book

HOW TO MAKE
PLAY DOUGH, BUBBLES,
MONSTER REPELLENT
AND MORE!

JENNIFER RADER
ILLUSTRATED BY BRIAN FOOTE

MAIN
STREET
BOOKS

DOUBLEDAY
New York London Toronto Sydney Auckland

A MAIN STREET BOOK
PUBLISHED BY DOUBLEDAY
a division of Bantam Doubleday Dell
Publishing Group, Inc.
1540 Broadway, New York, New York 10036

MAIN STREET BOOKS, DOUBLEDAY, and the portrayal
of a building with a tree
are trademarks of Doubleday, a division of
Bantam Doubleday Dell
Publishing Group, Inc.

Book design by Jennifer Ann Daddio

Library of Congress Cataloging-in-Publication Data

Rader, Jennifer, 1965—
The rainy day activity book : how to make play
dough, bubbles, monster repellent and more /
Jennifer Rader.
        p.   cm.
✓ 1. Handicraft—Juvenile literature.
    [1. Handicraft.]   I. Title.
    TT160.R33   1995
    ╱745.5—dc20
    94-27587
        CIP
        AC

ISBN 0-385-47544-6

First Edition

1 3 5 7 9 10 8 6 4 2

Contents

To Jared and Luke

Acknowledgements

I would like to thank my wonderful husband, Aaron, for his support and encouragement throughout the publication of this book, and especially for his suggestion to write this book.

In addition, I would also like to thank the following individuals for testing the recipes: Kim Chamberlain, Kathy Dougherty, Lori Elizares, Yvonne Hubert, Diana Rader, Lindsay Rader, Chris Shelby, and Lisa Stone.

Foreword

What began as a quick trip to the bookstore has culminated in this collection. I was looking for a book with recipes for bubbles, finger paint, and play dough. Recipes for the latter two recently published in a national magazine were far from adequate; no amount of stirring or kneading would ever make them work. I needed something for bubbles as well—my son, Jared, seemed to enjoy dumping the entire bottle of bubble solution as much as he enjoyed blowing the bubbles. Friends had books with these recipes and had given me a few titles as suggestions. The problem was that not one book had all three recipes. I could not believe it. Even trips to local libraries met with failure. Something needed to be done about this.

And so my research began. I collected and tested dozens of recipes. At the outset of research I decided that all recipes to be included in the book had to meet the following criteria: Ingredients were to be limited to those already in most homes or readily available at the supermarket—food products and soaps; the completed recipe was to be used in children's activities; and the result had to be *good*. Unlike most children's recipe books on the market, which included a few recipes for play dough, finger paint, and the like, this book was going to *focus* on recipes for activities. This was going to be *fun*.

The research for this book has been exciting. My sons have thoroughly enjoyed the various play dough, finger paint, and other recipes. And I have been free from worry, knowing that if Jared or his younger brother, Luke, did eat something, though it might leave a bad taste in his mouth, it certainly would not harm him. Most of the ingredients are items commonly eaten in our home.

It is my hope that the parents and children who purchase this book will enjoy the recipes and activities as much as my children and I have.

Disclaimer

Introduction

In contrast to many of the children's craft and recipe books on the market, *The Rainy Day Activity Book* is unique in that it focuses exclusively on recipes for children's activities—paints, play doughs, bubbles, and the like. It is specifically for children and their parents. Each recipe makes enough for two to three children, and most of the results can be saved for later use. All of the recipes utilize ingredients found in every home, or readily available at the supermarket, and all are nontoxic. However, this does not mean that the results are meant to be eaten. Quite the contrary. The recipes in this book (with the exception of those in Chapter 6), though made primarily from foods, do not taste good. They are nontoxic (not poisonous), and there is no need to worry if your child chooses to taste them, but chances are one taste will be sufficient.

The recipes in *The Rainy Day Activity Book* have been formulated to produce the best results possible without the use of additives or other chemicals. Following are some suggestions to help you achieve the same great results I did.

1. In all my recipes I have used paste food coloring rather than the liquids normally sold in little vials or bottles at the supermarket. While the latter work equally well in the recipes, paste food coloring is available in a wider range of colors, and the colors produced are much more vivid and intense. Paste coloring is available wherever cake decorating supplies are sold.

2. The finger paint and poster paint need to be stored in airtight containers when not in use. I have found that empty film containers are ideal for this purpose. They don't take up much space in the refrigerator, the top of the container can be painted to indicate the color inside, and your food containers remain available for their intended purpose. In addition, if the contents spoil, the container can be thrown away. Should you be in short supply of these handy containers, most film processing centers will be happy to save them for you.

3. In most of the recipes for modeling compounds, I have called for the salt to be added to boiling water rather than being mixed with the other dry ingredients. The purpose is to dissolve as much of the salt as possible in order to produce a smoother, nicer dough. If your children are helping make the dough, you may wish to substitute warm or hot tap water rather than risk having them near boiling water.

4. Alum, often used in pickling, is a preservative and is optional in the recipes that call for it. It can be toxic if ingested in large amounts (2 tablespoons or more). It is available in the spice section of most supermarkets and at pharmacies.

5. Glycerin is a colorless, syrupy liquid used in skin lotions, oral pharmaceuticals, and paste food coloring. It can cause vomiting, diarrhea, and nausea if taken in large amounts (1 tablespoon or more). It is available at pharmacies.

6. I have included a Notes section at the back of the book for you to record other recipes and ideas for activities that you may find.

7. And finally, *have fun!*

Chapter 1

Perfect Paints

Finger Paint

Yields approximately 2 cups.

1	package unflavored gelatin
1	cup boiling water
1/2	cup cornstarch
2	tablespoons sugar
1	cup cold water
	food coloring

Dissolve the gelatin in boiling water; set it aside. Combine the cornstarch, sugar and cold water in a saucepan over medium heat. Stir constantly until the mixture is slightly thickened. Remove the pan from heat, add the gelatin mixture and stir well. Pour the mixture into individual containers, and

18

add food coloring to each. If the mixture is too thin, return it to the stove or microwave it for a few seconds. Do not overcook. The paints can be stored for several weeks in airtight containers in the refrigerator. This will cause them to gel. Place the containers in hot water before using the gelled paints, and stir to restore smooth consistency.

Note: Use this paint on finger paint paper (or a heavy, glossy paper) for best results. You will be disappointed if you use this finger paint on regular paper.

This recipe makes about 2 cups of the paint. I usually make four colors at most and let the kids mix other colors on their paper so they learn that yellow and blue make green ... and I have fewer containers to clean up.

Poster Paint

Yields approximately 1/2 cup.

1/4	cup Finger Paint, after it has cooled
2	tablespoons water
3	tablespoons cornstarch
	food coloring

This paint works well on heavy paper and is ideal for finishing craft and ornament clays. (See Chapter 2.)

Mix all of the ingredients in a small bowl. Pour into individual containers and add food coloring to each. Store the paint in airtight containers in the refrigerator.

Milk Paint

Yields a little more than 1/2 cup.

3/4   cup powdered milk
1/2   cup water
    food coloring

Blend the milk and water in a blender. Pour into individual containers and add food coloring to each. Store the paint in airtight containers in the refrigerator. Milk paint must be used within a few days because the milk will spoil.

This paint dries quickly to a glossy, opaque finish.

Watercolors

Be sure to mix this concoction up a day before you plan to paint, since the paints will need to solidify before you begin

Yields 1 set of watercolors.

1	tablespoon white vinegar
1 1/2	tablespoons baking soda
1	tablespoon cornstarch
1/2	teaspoon glycerin
	food coloring

Mix the vinegar and baking soda in a small bowl, and allow it to foam. After the foaming stops, add the cornstarch and glycerin and stir very well, up to a few minutes. Portion the mixture into a paint palette, muffin tin or a similar container, and add food coloring. Make the colors dark, since drying and use will lighten them. Allow the watercolors to dry in a warm place for several hours or overnight.

To make Glitter Watercolors, add $^1/_2$ teaspoon fine glitter to the recipe before portioning into containers and adding the food coloring.

Squeeze-bottle Paint

Perfect for a quick activity.

Yields approximately 1 1/4 cups, enough for 3 to 4 squeeze bottles.

2   tablespoons all-purpose flour

3   tablespoons cold water

1   cup boiling water

2   tablespoons salt

     food coloring

Blend the flour and cold water in a small bowl until very smooth. Pour the boiling water into a medium bowl, add the flour mixture, and stir until smooth. Add the salt and stir. Pour the paint into small bowls and add a different food coloring to each. Pour the paint into squeeze-type bottles, such as empty glue bottles, and allow them to cool. Paint can then be used to make pictures. After your pictures are completed, shake extra salt onto them to make them glisten.

Egg Paint

Yields approximately $1/2$ cup.

2 tablespoons cornstarch

2 tablespoons water

3 egg yolks

food coloring

In a small bowl, mix the cornstarch into the water, then add the egg yolks and mix until well blended. Do not beat or you will have air bubbles in your paint. Pour the paint into film containers and add the food coloring. If necessary, thin the paints with water. They will keep for a few days stored in airtight containers in the refrigerator.

This paint dries to a glossy finish and is perfect for painting on plain paper. It also can be used to paint cookies and rolls before baking—anything that will be in the oven for only a short time.

Chapter 2
Play Clays

Play Dough

Yields approximately 1 1/2 cups.

1	cup boiling water
1/2	cup salt
1	cup all-purpose flour
1	tablespoon alum (optional)
1	tablespoon vegetable oil
	food coloring

Remove boiling water from the stove and add the salt. In a medium bowl, mix next three ingredients together, then add the salted water. When the dough is cool enough to handle comfortably, knead it until smooth, adding more flour if necessary. Divide the dough and knead in food coloring. This play dough lasts for months in airtight containers. If it dries out, add warm water a few drops at a time and knead the dough until it is pliable. To save your creations, simply allow them to air dry for a few days.

To make Sparkling Play Dough, add 1–2 tablespoons fine glitter to the play dough recipe.

To make Scented Play Dough, add 1–2 teaspoons vanilla extract (or use lemon for yellow, mint for green, peppermint for pink, etc.).

Bread Dough

This dough is particularly suited to making hanging ornaments and modeling play figures.

1/4   cup salt

1/2   cup boiling water

1   cup all-purpose flour

1/4   teaspoon vegetable oil

food coloring (optional)

Add the salt to the boiling water in a medium bowl. Then add the remaining ingredients and knead the dough to the desired consistency. Add the food coloring, if desired. Keep the dough wrapped in plastic when not in use. When modeling objects, keep a bowl of water nearby to moisten the dough and to smooth and attach parts. Bake at 300°F. for 45 to 60 minutes.

If you want to paint your bread dough creations, acrylic paint—found in most art supply stores—is both durable and attractive. Flat ornaments cut out of this dough will puff slightly during baking process. If the objects are not to be painted, consider brushing them with Egg Varnish (see p. 73) prior to baking.

Castles to Keep

Use this mixture to bring your castles inside as lasting reminders of summer's fun.

1   cup water

1/3   cup all-purpose flour

6   cups sand

Place the water and flour in a small saucepan. Cook over medium heat, stirring constantly, until thickened (about 2 minutes). Add this mixture to the sand in a large bowl, and stir to distribute. Using margarine and yogurt containers, cups, spoons, and other equipment, build a sand castle on a foil-covered piece of plywood, cutting board, or cookie sheet. Let it dry 1 day and then add toothpick-and-paper flags and people and animals modeled from Play Dough (see p. 28) or Bread Dough (see previous recipe).

Handprint Clay

This dough is ideal for making handprints (or footprints!) for grandparents and others. It dries very hard, so the handprint preserves well. This recipe will make two to three handprints. Let your children use the leftover dough to model other objects.

1/2   cup salt

3/4   cup boiling water

1   cup all-purpose flour

1   tablespoon cornstarch

1   teaspoon alum

Add the salt to the boiling water in a medium bowl and stir well. Add the remaining dry ingredients and knead thoroughly. On a lightly floured surface, roll the dough out to a thickness of approximately 1/4 inch. Using a bowl or plate as a pattern, cut out a circle of dough, and transfer the circle to

34

waxed paper. Place your child's hand on the dough circle. Press down each finger individually and then the palm of the hand. Dry the handprint at room temperature for several days. If desired, paint the handprint with acrylic paint when dry.

Jewelry Dough

This clay is ideal for making beads for necklaces. Other figures can also be made and then glued to barrettes or pin backs.

Yields approximately 3/4 cup.

6	tablespoons all-purpose flour
1/4	cup salt
1/4	cup cornstarch
1/4	cup warm water

Mix all the ingredients together in a medium bowl, and knead the mixture until it is smooth and not sticky, adding more water if necessary. Model beads and figures. Use a toothpick to make holes in the beads, and leave the toothpick in so that the

hole will not shrink. Allow your creations to dry 1 to 2 days. When dry, paint the jewelry with acrylic paint.

Ornament Clay

Although not much different from Craft Clay (see p. 40), this modeling compound is excellent for making ornaments. It dries to a pure white matte finish, or food coloring can be added to produce pastel shades.

Yields approximately 3 cups, enough for a few dozen ornaments.

2 cups baking soda

1 cup cornstarch

1 1/4 cups water

Cook all the ingredients in a saucepan over medium heat until the mixture is too thick to stir. When the dough has cooled enough to handle comfortably, knead it until smooth. Keep the dough wrapped in plastic when not in use.

Roll the dough out with a rolling pin to a thickness of approximately

$^1/_8$ inch. If the dough is much thicker, it will crack when drying; if it is much thinner, the ornament will warp. Cut the ornaments out with cookie cutters and carefully place them on a cookie sheet to dry. Use a straw to make holes in the ornaments so they can hang. Turn the ornaments several times during the drying process, which will take up to 2 days, depending on the size of the ornament and the humidity. Sand rough edges of the ornaments with sandpaper or an emery board, then paint them with acrylic or Poster Paint (see p. 20) or spray them with glitter.

Craft Clay

Yields approximately 3 cups, enough for several objects.

2	cups baking soda
1	cup cornstarch
$1^1/2$	cups water

Cook all the ingredients in a saucepan over medium heat until the mixture is too thick to stir. When the dough has cooled enough to handle comfortably, knead it until smooth. Keep the dough wrapped in plastic when not in use.

Objects made from this clay dry at room temperature within 1 to 2 days. Once dry, objects may be painted with acrylic or Poster Paint. (See p. 20.)

This is an extremely fine-grained clay suited for many art projects. It dries to a pure white matte finish.

Chapter 3

Good Clean Fun

A baby bottle is not only the perfect container for this, but it also makes the measuring easy!

Note: Glycerin, available at supermarket pharmacies, makes bubbles a little more durable. If your children are at a stage where they spill more than they blow, omit the glycerin.

Bubbles

Yields approximately 1 1/4 cups.

1 cup + 2 tablespoons (9 oz.) water

2 tablespoons (1 oz.) dish soap (Joy® or Dawn® works best)

1 tablespoon glycerin

Combine all the ingredients in a plastic bottle or jar with a top. Shake to mix the ingredients. For best results, allow the solution to sit a few hours before using.

Giant Bubbles

Yields approximately 4 1/4 cups.

3   cups water

1   cup dish soap (Joy® or Dawn® works best)

1/4 cup corn syrup

Combine all the ingredients in a medium bowl. Let the mixture sit for several hours before using. Pour the bubble solution into a frying pan and fashion a giant bubble wand from a wire coat hanger.

For best results, do this on a day when the humidity is high—the bubbles will be a lot bigger and will last a lot longer!

Bubble Bath

Yields approximately 1 5/8 cups.

1	cup liquid soap
1/2	cup mild, sudsy shampoo
1	tablespoon glycerin
1	tablespoon baby oil

Make this for yourself as well, adding some cologne for a special treat.

Note: To make tear-free bubble bath, simply use tear-free soap and shampoo.

Combine all the ingredients in a plastic bottle or jar with a top. Shake to mix the ingredients.

Soap Modeling

Yields 1/2 cup, enough for several small soaps.

1/2   cup laundry soap flakes

2   tablespoons hand lotion

     food coloring (optional)

Combine all the ingredients in a small bowl. Mix the mixture with your fingertips until the lotion is well distributed. Model the soap into simple figures or press it into candy molds. Let dry 1 to 2 days.

Make some little "friends" to entice your child into the tub.

Note: If you don't have laundry soap flakes, you can use a carrot peeler to make them from a bar of soap.

Bath Paint

2   tablespoons liquid soap
    food coloring

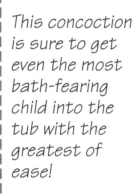

This concoction is sure to get even the most bath-fearing child into the tub with the greatest of ease!

Portion the soap into several containers and add food coloring to make pastel shades. Let children paint the tub and themselves as they bathe. These bath paints rinse easily off the children, the tub, the walls, and you!

Chapter 4

Disguises

Scar Tissue

Yields 2 tablespoons, enough scar tissue for several children.

1   package unflavored gelatin
2   tablespoons hot water
    red food coloring (optional)
    baby powder

Place the gelatin in a small bowl. Add the water and stir. When the gelatin thickens, apply it with a spatula or fingertip to resemble scar tissue. Dust on baby powder to resemble skin. If desired, microwave remaining scar tissue for a few seconds to thin it, and add red food coloring. Apply the dripping red gelatin to resemble blood and guts.

Use this concoction to transform your angels into ghouls and goblins for Halloween.

Brown Greasepaint

Yields $1/2$ teaspoon, enough for 1 to 2 children.

$1/2$ teaspoon shortening

1 teaspoon cocoa

In a small bowl, microwave the shortening for 10 to 15 seconds on high to soften it. Mix in the cocoa with a fingertip. Apply to the face with fingertips.

Excellent for making bears and puppy dogs.

49

White Greasepaint

Yields 2 teaspoons, enough for 3 to 4 children.

1 teaspoon shortening

1 teaspoon Desitin®

    food coloring (optional)

    baby powder

In a small bowl, microwave the shortening for 10 to 15 seconds on high to soften it. Mix in the Desitin® with a fingertip. Add food coloring, if desired. Apply the greasepaint to the face with fingertips. If necessary, dust on baby powder to set the paint.

Use this all year 'round for clowns and animals.

NOTE: IF YOU DON'T HAVE ANY DESITIN® OR YOU ARE CONCERNED THAT YOUR CHILDREN WILL EAT THE GREASE-PAINT, THE FOLLOWING RECIPE ALSO WORKS WELL.

Yields 1 teaspoon, enough for 1 to 2 children.

1   teaspoon shortening
2   teaspoons powdered sugar
     food coloring (optional)

In a small bowl, microwave the shortening for 10 to 15 seconds on high to soften it. Mix in the sugar with a fingertip. Add food coloring, if desired. Proceed on previous page.

Face Paint

Yields approximately $1/4$ cup, enough for several children.

$1\,1/2$	teaspoons cornstarch
$3/4$	teaspoon face cream
2	teaspoons water
	food coloring

This face paint is not the one usually found at school carnivals and fairs. It is thinner, and the colors aren't generally as intense, allowing you to achieve some very interesting effects. And, unlike most of the children's face paint on the market, this face paint won't rub off onto clothes or furniture!

Mix the cornstarch and face cream in a small bowl with a fingertip. Add the water. Portion the mixture into small containers (such as a paint palette or muffin tin) and add food coloring. Apply with a fine paintbrush.

Chapter 5

Sticky Stuff

Glue

Children can use this glue for their art projects, and clean-up is a breeze!

Yields approximately 1/4 cup.

1	package unflavored gelatin
1/4	cup boiling water
1	tablespoon white vinegar
1	teaspoon glycerin

Place the gelatin and boiling water in a small bowl. Stir constantly until the gelatin is completely dissolved. Add the vinegar and glycerin, and stir until blended. Cool and pour into a squeeze bottle. This glue will gel. To restore consistency, simply microwave it for a few seconds or place it in hot water until the glue is liquid again.

Sticker Solution

Yields 2 teaspoons of sticker solution,
enough for dozens of stickers.

1   teaspoon flavored gelatin
2   teaspoons boiling water

Place the gelatin and boiling water in a small bowl. Stir constantly until the gelatin is completely dissolved. Let the mixture cool 1 minute. While the sticker solution is warm, brush a thin coat on the back of each cut-out stamp with a finger. Allow the stamps to dry for 1 day. When dry, lick them and stick them to paper or glass.

Cut out pictures from a glossy magazine and other sources, too, such as your children's own drawings, before making this solution.

57

Paste

Yields approximately 1 cup.

2   tablespoons all-purpose flour

2   tablespoons sugar

2   tablespoons water

1/2   teaspoon alum (optional—acts as a preservative)

3/4   cup water

Mix the flour, sugar, 2 tablespoons water, and alum, if desired, in a small bowl until completely smooth. Bring the 3/4 cup water to a boil in a small saucepan, and add the contents of the bowl. Reduce the heat to medium and cook for 10 to 15 minutes, stirring frequently. Cool the paste and place it in an airtight container. This paste will last for several weeks if stored in the refrigerator.

Colored Rice or Macaroni

Make them both for great collages.

1   teaspoon water

     food coloring

1/2   cup rice or macaroni

Mix the water and food coloring in a plastic container with a lid or in a zipper sandwich bag. Add the rice or macaroni and shake to distribute the color. Dry the rice or macaroni on newspaper for several hours or overnight. Repeat the recipe to make other colors. Use the rice or macaroni to make collages and pictures on paper.

Colored Crushed Eggshells

1/4   teaspoon vinegar

        food coloring

1   teaspoon crushed eggshells

Make several different colors at once and save to use on a rainy day!

Mix the vinegar and food coloring in a small container and add the eggshells. Allow them to soak until you achieve the desired shade. Then drain off the dye and pour the egg-shells onto newspaper to dry. Repeat the recipe to make other colors. Squeeze glue into a pattern on the paper and

sprinkle on eggshells. Lift the paper and gently shake off the excess eggshells. Repeat this procedure with other colors of eggshells to make a complete picture.

Papier-mâché

Yields approximately 1 1/2 cups.

1/2   cup all-purpose flour

1   cup warm water

Place the flour in a small bowl. Add the water gradually, mixing continuously to prevent lumps from forming. Use this concoction liberally to paste newspaper strips to balloons, toilet paper tubes, newspaper balls and so on. Allow your sculpture to dry for several days. If the weather is humid or cool, add 1 teaspoon salt to the recipe to retard mold formation. When dry, finish your project with Poster Paint (see p. 20), tempera and/or Bread Dough (see p. 30).

Use this concoction to make masks, piñatas, jewelry, more!

Colored Salt or Sand

2   tablespoons salt or sand
    food coloring

Place the salt or sand in a small container with a lid. Add the food coloring and shake to distribute the color. Repeat the recipe to make other colors. Glue your colored salt or sand onto paper.

Chapter 6

Tummy Yummies

Animal Bread

Yields approximately 2 dozen animals.

1	tablespoon (1 package) active dry yeast
1/4	cup lukewarm water
1/4	cup butter
1	teaspoon salt
1/4	cup sugar
1	cup milk
1	egg
4	cups all-purpose flour
	raisins, almonds, cloves, etc., for eyes

Don't make too many of these, or they might be the only things your children will eat!

68

In a large bowl, sprinkle the yeast over lukewarm water and let it ferment for 10 minutes. Add all the remaining ingredients, except flour and raisins, and mix well. Gradually add enough flour to make a medium-soft dough. Cover the bowl with a clean, damp towel and set it in warm place to rise, until doubled in volume, approximately 45 minutes. After the dough has risen, punch it down, knead it briefly and shape as desired. Allow the shapes to rise a second time. Brush on egg wash (recipe follows) and bake at 375°F. for 20 minutes.

You can use almost any bread dough recipe, except recipes for French bread or very sweet dough.

The following are some suggestions for making animals, or you can use your imagination and have fun with your own designs. If something slips off during baking, use egg wash to stick it back together, or use a toothpick or raw spaghetti noodles.

Anteater/Alligator: Roll out a long body with a fat middle and skinny ends. Pull out folds for eyelids and add eyes. Roll out ropes for legs and attach them on the bottom. (Stop here for an anteater.) Make a jaw and attach it on the bottom. Put aluminum foil in the mouth to keep the jaws separated. After the bread has risen 10 to 15 minutes, use kitchen scissors to cut scales and nostrils.

Caterpillar: Make lots of little balls and stick them together. Use cloves or raisins to put a face on the head. For antennae, use toothpicks or raw spaghetti and put little balls on top.

Dinosaur: Start with a ball of dough. Narrow it out at both ends. Make the jaw as for the alligator, and add eyes. Roll out ropes for legs and attach them on the bottom. Cut three large scales around the neck after the dough has risen 10 to 15 minutes.

Hedgehog or porcupine (also pinecones, Christmas trees): Start with a ball of dough. Narrow out a snout 1 $^1/2$ inches long. Cut lots of little scales all over the body with kitchen scissors. Add eyes and cut a little mouth as well.

Ladybug: Start with a flat, oblong ball of dough. Attach a smaller ball of dough for the head. Make a line for the wings. Roll out tiny balls of dough for spots.

Pig: Start with a flat ball of dough. Make ears chocolate kiss-shaped and attach. Make a flat ($^1/8$—$^1/4$ inch) circle for the nose. Make deep eye sockets close to the nose with a fingertip. Roll out little balls for the eyes and place them in the sockets. Use a straw or butter knife to make the nostrils.

Snail: Roll out a long rope of dough and coil it up.

Spider: Start with a flat ball of dough. Attach a smaller ball of dough for the head. Roll out ropes for legs and attach them underneath.

Turtle: Start with a flat ball of dough. Roll out ropes for legs and a little tail. Add a small oblong head. Attach everything on the bottom. Web the feet and mark the shell with a sharp knife.

Egg Varnish

1   egg, beaten

Brush the egg with a pastry brush onto dough ornaments prior to baking.

Egg Wash

1   egg white, beaten

Brush on egg white with a pastry brush prior to baking.

Cookie Play Dough

Perfect for making holiday treats. Use Cookie Paint (see p. 78) for more decorating fun.

Yields 2 to 3 dozen cookies.

1	cup butter
2/3	cup sugar
2/3	cup corn syrup
2	teaspoons vanilla
1	egg, beaten
4	cups all-purpose flour
2	teaspoons baking powder
	food coloring (optional)

Place the butter, sugar, and corn syrup in a saucepan. Cook the mixture over medium heat, stirring, until the butter is melted and the sugar is dis-

solved. Remove the pan from the heat, add the vanilla and cool for 5 minutes. Add the egg. In a separate bowl, combine the flour and baking powder, then add the flour mixture to the butter mixture and knead. Color the dough, if desired, and chill 2 hours or overnight. Shape the dough by hand, or roll it out, cut it with cookie cutters, and decorate it with small pieces of different-color dough. Bake on an ungreased cookie sheet at 350°F. for 8 to 10 minutes. Remove the shapes immediately and cool them on wire racks.

Cookie Puppets

Yields approximately ten 3- to 4-inch puppets.

1/3	cup shortening
1/3	cup butter
1/2	cup sugar
1/4	cup brown sugar
1	egg
1	teaspoon vanilla
1 3/4	cups all-purpose flour
1	teaspoon baking powder
1/2	teaspoon salt
1/2	teaspoon each allspice, cinnamon, ginger, and nutmeg

In a large bowl, beat the shortening, butter, sugars, egg and vanilla. Sift the dry ingredients together and add them to the butter mixture. Cover the dough and refrigerate it for 1 to 2 hours. Mold the puppets freehand or use cookie cutters as patterns. Be sure to make the puppets no thicker than $1/2$ inch. (If the puppet is too thick, the edges will burn before the center is done.) Place the puppets on an ungreased cookie sheet 2 inches apart. Insert a craft stick 1 to 2 inches into the base of each puppet. Bake at 375°F. for 12 to 15 minutes. Decorate the puppets with Cookie Paint (see p. 78) or frosting when cooled.

Cookie Paint

This "paint" is perfect for Cookie Play Dough (see p. 74), Cookie Puppets (see p. 76), and Gingerbread Puzzles (see p. 82).

Yields approximately 1/2 cup.

2   cups powdered sugar, sifted

1   tablespoon corn syrup

2   tablespoons milk

    food coloring

In a large bowl, stir together the first three ingredients to make a smooth glaze. Add more milk, if necessary. Pour small amounts of the glaze onto flat cookies to make a "canvas" and allow to dry, about 1 hour. After all the cookies have been covered, add a few drops of milk to the remaining glaze to thin. Pour small amounts of cookie paint into a muffin tin and stir in food coloring. Apply the cookie paint with a paintbrush.

Pretzel Fun

Yields approximately 2 dozen pretzels.

1	tablespoon (1 package) active dry yeast
1/2	cup lukewarm water
2	eggs, beaten
1/2	cup vegetable oil
1	cup milk
1	teaspoon salt
5	cups all-purpose flour
1/4	cup sugar
1	egg, beaten
2	tablespoons coarse salt

Great for a winter afternoon activity-treat.

In a large bowl, dissolve the yeast in lukewarm water and whisk in the eggs, oil, and milk. Add the dry ingredients

to make a soft dough. Knead 5 minutes, until the dough is smooth. Roll pieces of the dough into ropes about $1/2$ inch in diameter and 18 to 24 inches long. Form various shapes—pretzels, hearts, butterflies, cars and trucks and the like. Making children's initials is also fun. Place the shapes on greased baking sheets. Brush the tops of the shapes with the beaten egg and sprinkle with salt. Bake the shapes immediately at 425°F. for 12 to 15 minutes.

For a chewier pretzel, drop the shaped dough into boiling water. When the dough floats to the top, remove it. Brush with egg and sprinkle with coarse salt, then bake at 400° F. for 20 minutes on greased baking sheets.

81

Gingerbread Puzzles

Yields 2 to 3 puzzles.

2 1/2	cups all-purpose flour
1	teaspoon baking soda
1/2	teaspoon salt
1	teaspoon ginger
1	teaspoon cinnamon
1/2	teaspoon nutmeg
1/2	teaspoon cloves
1/2	cup shortening
1/2	cup sugar
1/2	cup molasses
1	egg, beaten

In a large bowl, mix the dry ingredients and set them aside. In a small bowl, soften the shortening in the microwave on high for 15 to 20 seconds. Add the sugar, molasses, and egg to the shortening and blend well. Add this mixture to the dry ingredients and knead until well mixed. Roll dough out on a lightly floured board until it is $1/8$ to $1/4$ inch thick. Cut the dough into sections as large as you can handle, up to 8 by 8 inches. Transfer the dough to a cookie sheet and bake at 350°F. for 8 to 10 minutes. Remove from the oven and cut into pieces immediately, using one cookie cutter (gingerbread man, star, heart, etc.) as a pattern for the center piece, pressing down just enough to make an imprint, and then cutting the pattern and surrounding pieces

with knife. Allow the puzzle to finish cooling on the cookie sheet. For
best results, keep the puzzle simple.

Decorator Icing

Yields approximately 1/2 cup.

2 tablespoons milk

2 tablespoons light corn syrup

2 cups powdered sugar, sifted

In a small bowl, mix together the liquid ingredients and then add them to the sugar. Use immediately. This icing dries to a hard, shiny finish that is perfect for icing gingerbread puzzles.

You don't have to sift sugar from a freshly opened 2-pound bag.

Peanut Butter Play Dough

Make sure the kids have had lunch first!

Yields approximately 3/4 cup, enough for 2 to 3 children.

1/3 cup peanut butter

1/4 cup honey

1/2 cup powdered milk

Knead all the ingredients together in a medium bowl. Children can model simple figures and eat as they play.

Colored Sugar

1   tablespoon sugar
    food coloring

Shake the sugar and food coloring together in a plastic bag to distribute the color. Repeat the recipe to make other colors.

Sprinkle this on top of the icing of the gingerbread puzzles.

Easter Egg Dye

food coloring

1 teaspoon vinegar

1/2 cup boiling water

Place a generous amount of food coloring in a cup and then add vinegar and water. Allow hard-boiled eggs to sit in the dye for a few minutes, depending on the intensity of color desired. Repeat the recipe to make other colors.

With the wide range of paste colors available, why limit yourself to the high-priced Easter kits?

Chapter 7

Other important Stuff

Gelatin Plastic

This "plastic" can be cut with scissors to make doll dishes, sequins and the like. Pieces also can be threaded and hung in a sunny place, to look like panes of stained glass, birds or colored snowflakes.

2 packages unflavored gelatin
6 tablespoons boiling water
   food coloring

Place the gelatin and boiling water in a small bowl, and stir until the gelatin is completely dissolved. Add food coloring. Pour the mixture into plastic lids (such as large margarine or coffee can lids) and allow it to dry 1 to 2 days. Remove the Gelatin Plastic from the lid when its edges are dry and the center is still pliable. Repeat the recipe to make other colors.

Monster Repellent

1/2 cup water

few drops cologne, food coloring and/or some essential oils

Combine ingredients in a spray bottle and set the bottle on "mist." The spray really does chase monsters away!

The perfect solution for those poor children who have goblins under their beds at night. This spray will take care of the little monsters!

Eggshell Chalk

Yields 1 stick of chalk.

Ideal for hopscotch!

4—5   eggshells

1   teaspoon flour

1   teaspoon very hot tap water

    food coloring (optional)

Wash and dry the eggshells, then grind them to powder on clean, smooth concrete using a smooth rock (or inside with a smooth rock and steel bowl). Sweep up the powder and place it in a bowl, discarding any large pieces of shell. Place the flour and hot water in another bowl and add 1 tablespoon eggshell powder, mixing until a paste forms. Add food coloring, if desired. Shape and press the mixture firmly into the shape of a chalk stick, and roll the stick up tightly in a strip of paper towel. Allow to dry approximately 3 days, until hard. Remove the paper towel. Use Eggshell Chalk for sidewalks only.

Dog Biscuits

Yields approximately 3 dozen treats.

2 1/2	cups whole wheat flour
2 ~~1~~	eggs
6	tablespoons bacon grease *(or ham grease and lard)*
1/2	cup powdered milk
1	teaspoon brown sugar
1/2	teaspoon garlic powder *(or 1/2 tsp. Parmesan cheese)*
1/2	teaspoon salt
1/2	cup cold water

In a large bowl, knead together all the ingredients, then roll the dough out to $^1/4$-inch thick. Model bone-shaped treats, use cookie cutters or simply cut into squares with a knife. Place the treats on an ungreased cookie sheet and bake at 350°F. for 30 minutes.

Chapter 8

Cleaning Up

Wet Wipes

Perfect for cleaning up after projects or for baby's bottom.

2   cups water

2   tablespoons baby shampoo

1   tablespoon baby oil

    small pieces of rags

Mix together the liquid ingredients in an airtight container and add the rags.

Window Cleaner

1/2 teaspoon liquid soap

3 tablespoons vinegar

2 cups water

Place the ingredients in a spray bottle and use in place of commercial window cleaner.

It doesn't work quite as well as cleaners with ammonia, but it's perfectly safe for children who love to "kiss" the window.

Wood Cleaner

2   tablespoons food-grade linseed or walnut oil

2   tablespoons vinegar

1/4   cup lemon juice

Place all the ingredients in a glass jar. Using a soft cloth, rub the cleaner into wood until it is clean. If you want to save any leftover wood cleaner, add a few drops of vitamin E as a preservative, and cover the jar tightly.

Floor Cleaner

2   tablespoons liquid soap

2   gallons hot water

a few drops of pine oil

Place the ingredients in a bucket and mop as usual.

NOTES

NOTES

NOTES